AF225721

Acknowledgements

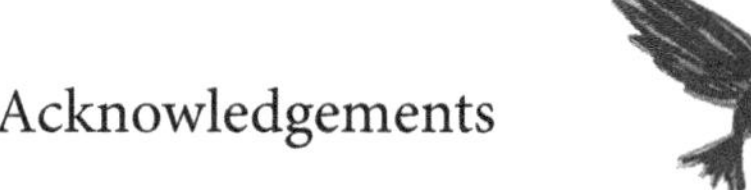

Phyllis Lankshear
The poet who nurtured my creativity.
Nan, you are eternally missed.

Bronte & Ruby
I'm so incredibly proud of your sisterhood.
Kind, resilient and wise beyond your years.
Fly my baby birds.
"feel the breeze as you begin to soar"
Love you always & forever.

Mim
Thank you for your endless support and
editorial eyes. I love sharing my work with you.

Andy - My Love
Silent witness and co-conspirator
in our flawed, humanly messy love story.
It's been a journey.

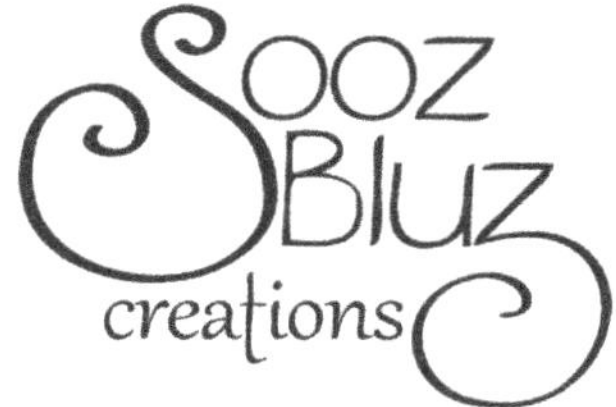

Caged, Clipped & Cabinet Filed

Susie Sotiropoulos

Little Bird

Fairytales and the white dress of silk
Falsify reality to disguise sour milk
Sweet talk of love and real partnership
Lured me to accept his bargaining chip

Sing little bird sing

Naive little I, stepped into the cage
Bound to a life where he sets the stage
Restless wings, batter hard steel
Every day trapped is how I feel

Sing little bird sing

The bonds of love with each new babe
Blissfully distract from the unfair trade
As I nurture, guide and completely adore
Career path melts through the floor

Sing little bird sing

Another load, another dish
Why was this the predetermined wish?
Unconsciously trained to accept a role
With stolen power that fades my soul

Sing little bird sing

Whispers echo through my head
Sting each time I hear it said
"Oh poor man, he works so hard"
But my endless labour? A disregard

Sing little bird sing

My children grow in love and grace
And I try to carve a little space
With a role beyond wife, mother, house
To be robbed by my conditioned spouse

Sing little bird sing

The poison pulses through my vein
This unyielding patriarchal reign
Disempowerment is preprogrammed
To keep us fighting with just one hand

Sing little bird sing

The cage is here, the steel is brutal
Wings are broken, but my voice is crucial
So...

Sing little bird sing

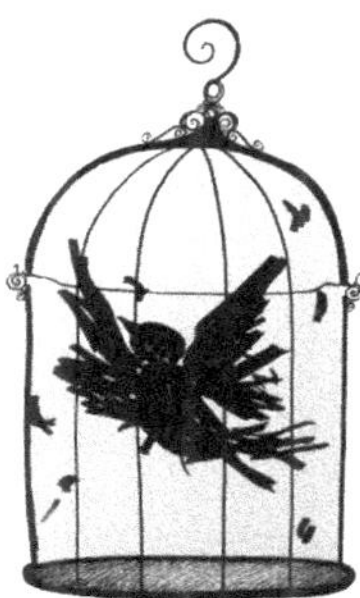

Geometric Design

In deep empty spaces
I breathe in your smoke
Burn out my lungs
Cry fire as I choke

Body fuelled rapture
A perpendicular line
Impaled through my heart
Your geometric design

A sweet romantic rush
Dark eyes pierced my skin
But swiftly turned the corner
Denied access in

You drove through my horizon
Smudged the edges as you went
Cruised to your vanishing point
A fool's heartache I lament

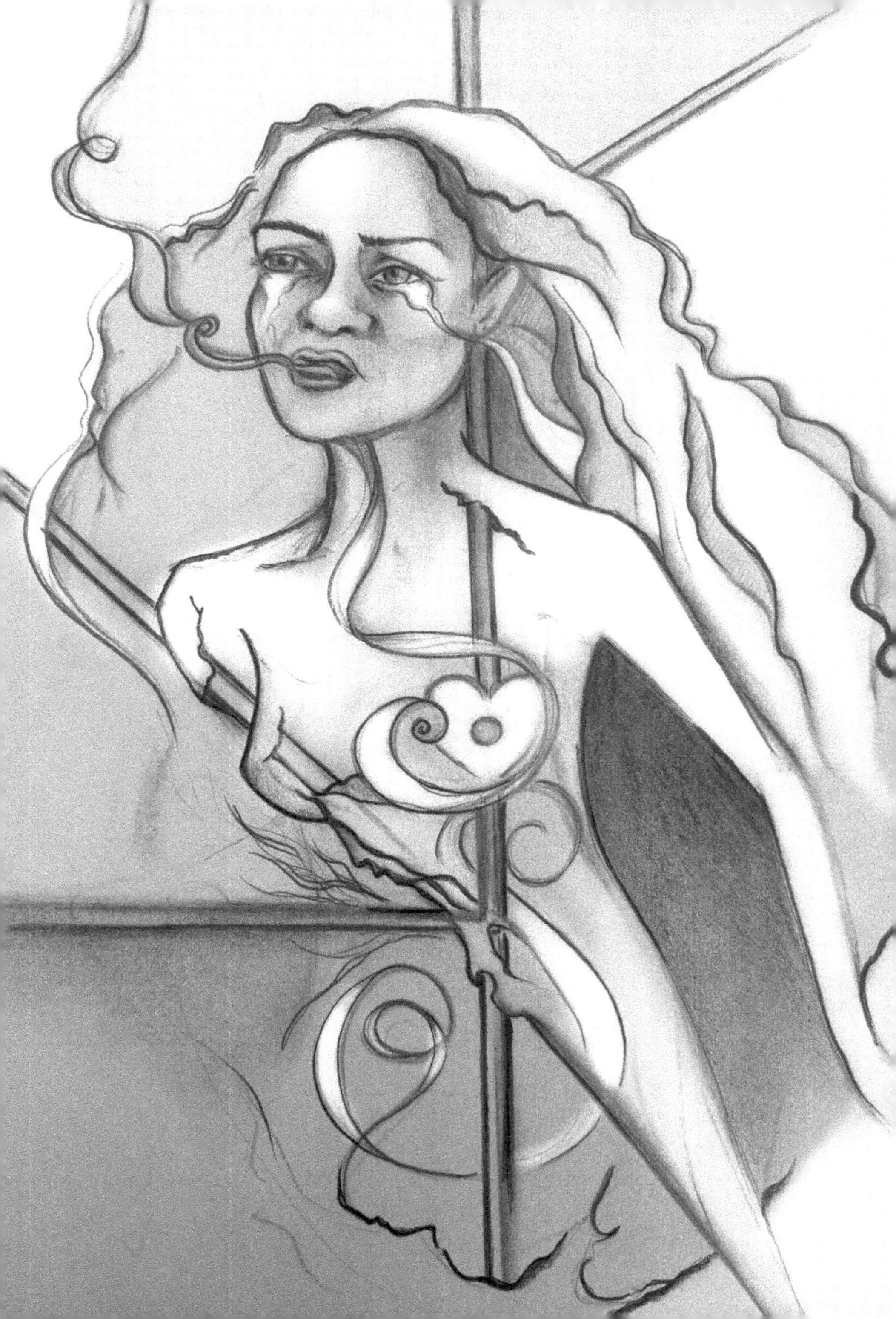

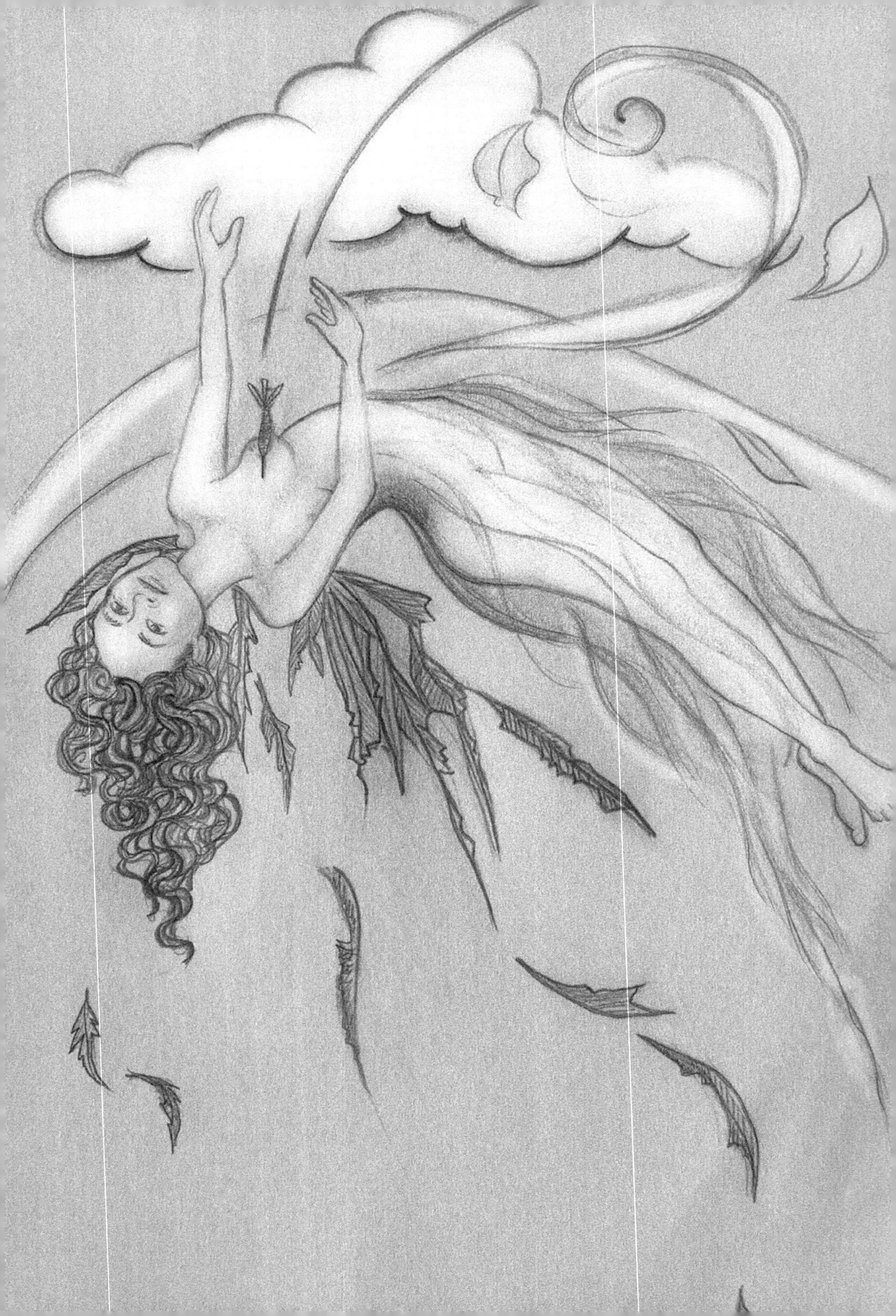

Speared

Yours from the moment I saw your grin
And the desire in your eyes
Swept up, I'm an autumn leaf
Wonder filled my wild wind skies

Crazy high and love sublime
Greedy writes the second line
Floating lover, don't let me fall
From the façade of your cloud nine

You wanted the glossy cover
Loved the romance and the chase
But once the book was opened
Disappeared without a trace

A fallen angel has no wings
When you wield a deadly dart
Screaming down the surging pain
Breathing life, she healed my heart

False Revelry

Christmas lights still blink
As the crowd cries in cheer
Jubilant hugs and kisses
What a fabulous new year

A collective annual reset
Lists of how we will do better
Ignite my internal time bomb
Panic fuelled climatic weather

January lights the fuse
What path will I choose?

Fear of failure keeps me stagnant
Irony sings at my chronic flaw
This eternal indecision
Paints bile on my wall

Be brave I tell my diary
But coward-ess takes my call
If you take a leap and jump
You know you'll only fall!

Fear is my enemy
Standing at the gate
Whispers on the wind
Seals the tomb of my fate

I hear my frail voice
Echoing within
Boxed by indecision
The year repeats my sin

Going Nowhere

Angry at myself
Wasting away at home
Angry at my partner
For making this my zone

Solitude and silence
Soaks the space in red
Confidence grows smaller
Unsure which way to tread

Passive aggressive behaviour
Filling up my head
As I follow the same old road
That walks on the spot instead

Bleak Repeat

I yawn, time trickles
And sand slowly falls
Like drying paint
On stark white walls

The numbness of feeling
Seeps to the bone
Monotonous conversation
Incessant buzzing drone

I need energy and colour
Composed creatively
This loop of bleak repeat
Is slowly killing me

Where Are You?

In a quiet moment
I glimpse the spark of you
A light that wraps my heart
In warmth and love so true

Too fleeting is that feeling
Before demons shut your door
Stone grey and heavy
Heart bleeding on the floor

Disengaged from living
Rat running on the spot
Eyes glazed and vacant
Anger churns a knot

I know you feel cheated
Chained to obligation
Can't find the trigger
For a new destination

But head against walls
Only bruise and bleed
Defeated you remain
Ignored is your need

The misery you harbour
Eradicates your light
'Til only glimpses shine
Of heart's pure delight

Hiding In My Sweater

I am skin deep filtered emotion
Can't face demons swarming beneath
So I cheat the system and try to release them
As burning bile shatters forth
A surging river flows
Swift and violent from my core
But all I feel is sweet release
Before you knock upon my door

I want to open a window
And scramble through its frame
Reality takes a swing at me
When I try to play this game

In sweet rare moments
Free of heavy chains
Your heart feels so beautiful
Rekindles our dying flame
Answers an echo I once knew
I want to try and love you more
The way I know you want me to

The façade is fading fast now
Can't hide in my own skin
It's a raging fire
And fear smokes within
So I'll pull on my warm sweater
Hide the mess I've been making
Comfort my inner child
Until the cycle repeats again

You're autotuned to duty
Programmed from mother's womb
I'm pleading, begging, screaming
Can't get through your cocoon
I crawl inside my heart
I cannot try anymore
You won't even notice
It's me who keeps the score

Your luggage is too heavy
The zipper teeth are stuck
I am marrow damaged
A tortured sitting duck

Poisonous Choices

The night silence is broken
With a heavy weighted sigh
He breathes deeply in
Noisy air exhales from his nostrils
The sound of passive aggression
Lingers
Like poison polluting the air
"My life is torture"
He says loudly
Intending to be heard
What is there to say?
You created it by your choices
You've been heeding the wrong voices
I begged you for years
Cried rivers of tears
Now live with the consequences
Cos I'm finally numb to barbed wire fences
Instead she says nothing
Rolls close to the edge
Pretends to be sleeping
As he breathes deeply in

Bystander

Still searching for the key
To unlock this cage
But wrestle with my fury
And its ineffective rage

I know I'm a bystander
In my own life
As I listen to my fear
Cutting like a knife

A traitor to my passion
And creativity
Veiled family duty
Its weight my gravity

The conflict in my head
Won't leave me alone
A drowning sea of words
I sink like a stone

Muted

Stone statue silent
The talker lost her words
The vibrating hum of letters and sounds
That cascade like a roaring waterfall
Stilled
Not even a trickle
No flow
Just the faint feeling of air slowly exhaling
Inhaling

Not stumped for lack of argument
Nor meaningful thoughts to say
But silenced by the knowledge
They are unheard either way

statue silent stone statue silent stone statue silent
stone statue silent stone statue silent stone stat
silent stone statue silent stone statue silent ston
statue silent stone statue silent stone statue silent
stone statue silent stone statue silent stone sta
silent stone statue silent stone statue silent ston
statue silent   stone statue silent st
stone sta   silent stone statue
silent st   statue silent stone
statue   silent stone sta
stone   statue silent s
silent   stone stat
statue   silent st
stone   statue sil
silent   stone sta
statue   silent st
stone   statue sil
                                 silent sto
                                 statue siler
                                 stone stat
                                 silent

the talker lost her words

Hourglass

Downward tumbling and moving fast
She spiralled through the hourglass
Time was up with nothing changed
Face planted, badly deranged
A tangled mess and broken façade
Life ambitio[illegible] and marred
Time trapp[illegible]ally flipped
Falling, fa[illegible]er sanity slipped

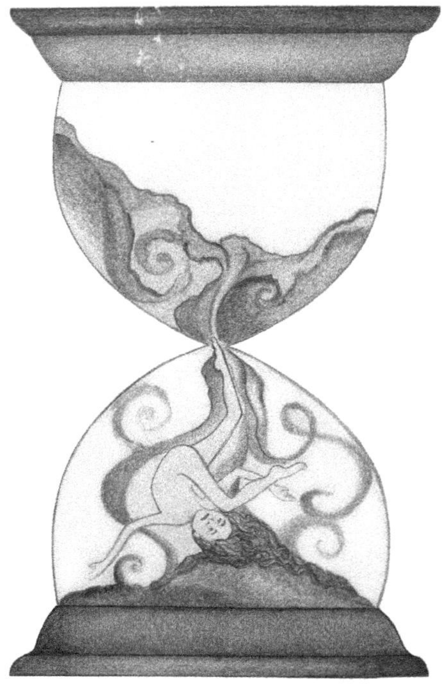

Whose Wonderland

Each unspoken demand
Every sleight of the hand
Tumbles me down the hole

Time keeps ticking
Their lies k[illegible]ng
I cry for the h[illegible]ole

I get used to the se[illegible]g
To appease I'm betting
But I spin out of control

White rabbit is racing
And I'm tired of chasing
Madness is the new role

Porcelain

I pretended not to notice
How truly I was broken
'Til my child held the mirror
It could not be unspoken

Years of disappointment
Carrying too much load
Screaming on the inside
Surface smile paved my road

Monotony droned his silence
Disengagement was his call
As I raged in furious anguish
Rain stained my greying wall

Every unfulfilled promise
Every deadlines' further delay
Anger fuelled my body
'Til I was skin covered decay

Pretty painted flowers
Once adorned this porcelain
Faded, cracked and shattered
Thinning glaze holds it within

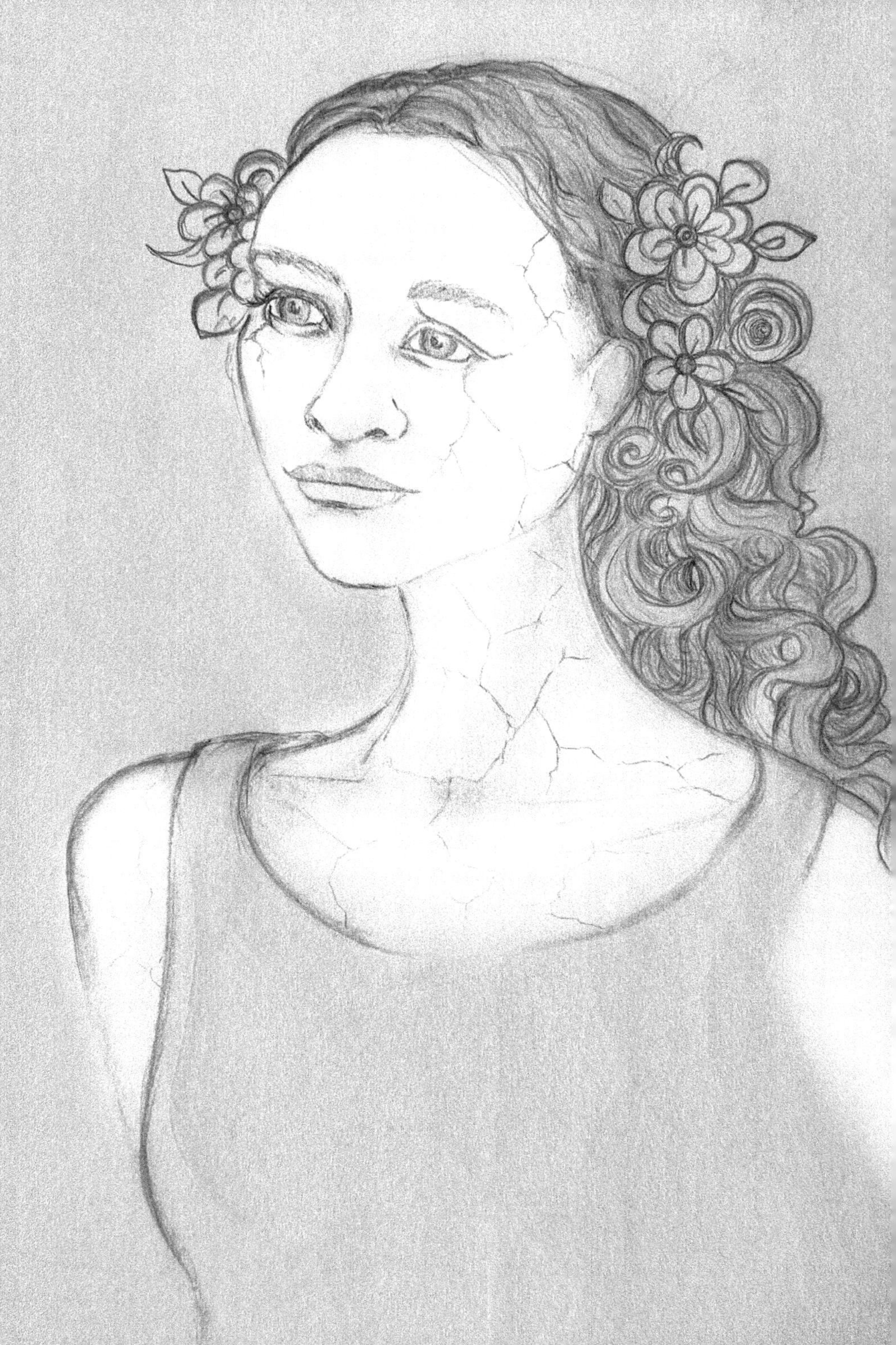

Achilles Heel

I don't know what you see
when you look into my eyes
As I try to mask the loathing
and the choice I now despise
The sun keeps ever setting
on the same blue destination
Changing miraged roads
to dark snakes of reflection

Small balls of luminous light
hang high along the street
A line of delicate dancers
Recall thoughts soft and sweet
My hands flinch and curl
around the steering wheel
Memories are rose-tinted
My cruel Achilles heel

As they shimmer and uncoil
Then slowly disappear
Singing ever sweetly
Lullabies in my ear
Blindly, seeking rapture
A spiritual hallucination
I sidestep monotony
blur truth with imagination

I pull into the driveway
Cut the engine and revery
Push steel in the front door
Deeply breathe and turn the key
We retouch and change history
Bathe in glistening sunshine
To blind current reality
Let it sink in velvet wine

I step inside our walls
You scroll across your screen
Politely greet each other
Formal, sterile, bored and clean
You resume the mindless tapping
I find the girls and kiss my dears
Join in their bonded banter
Wipe freshly streaming tears

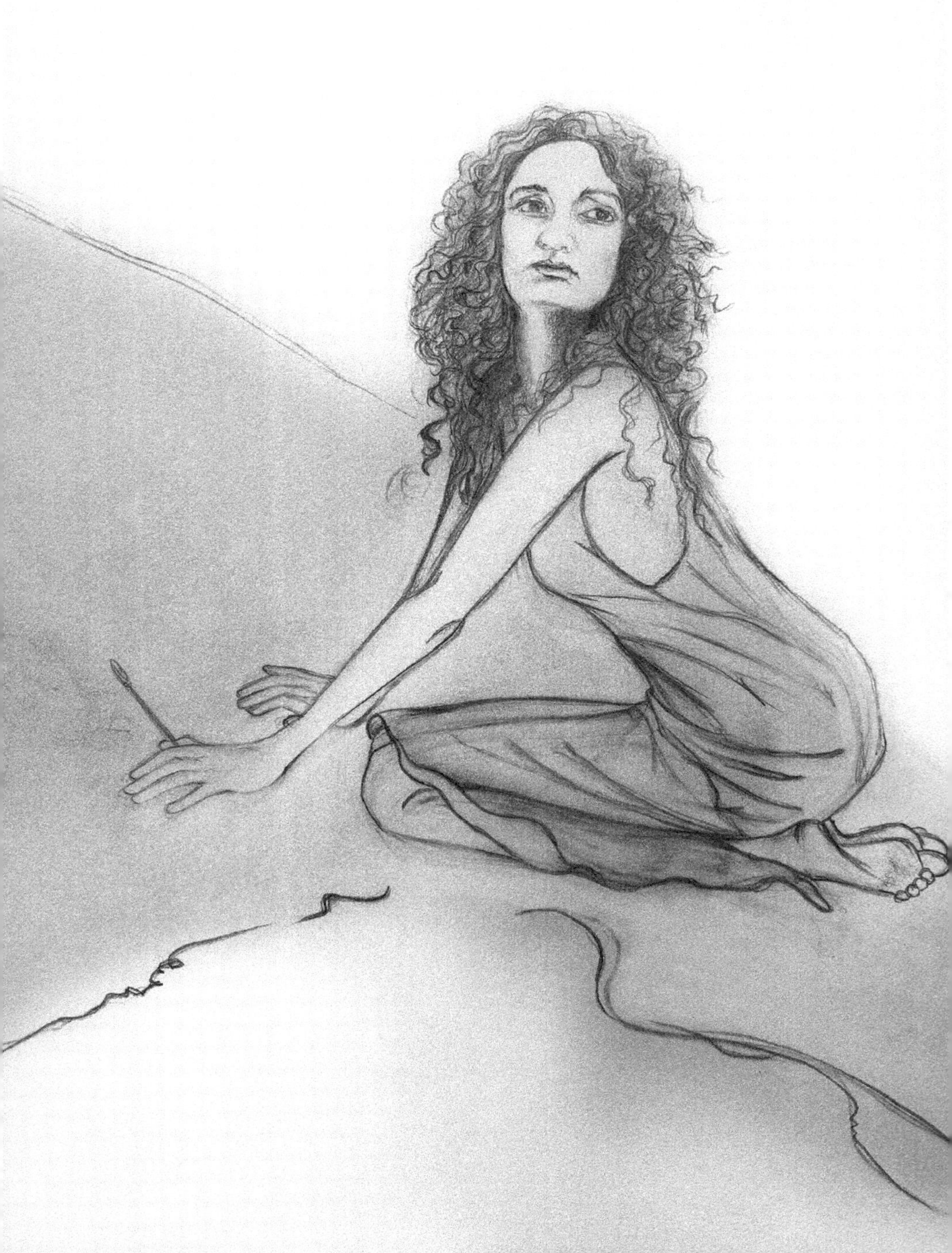

Caught Between Extremes

Feeling like an animal locked in a cage
Pacing with fire, surging with rage
Frenzy soon retires to exhausted retreat
Bars burn emotion to broken down defeat
Bound between anger and disassociation
Teeth bared snarls or empty resignation

In the absence of connection
There is solitary reflection
Drifting down memories, the laneway of time
Re-brush the echo like polishing a dime
As present hollowness, fills up her head
She dreamily sings each brushstroke instead

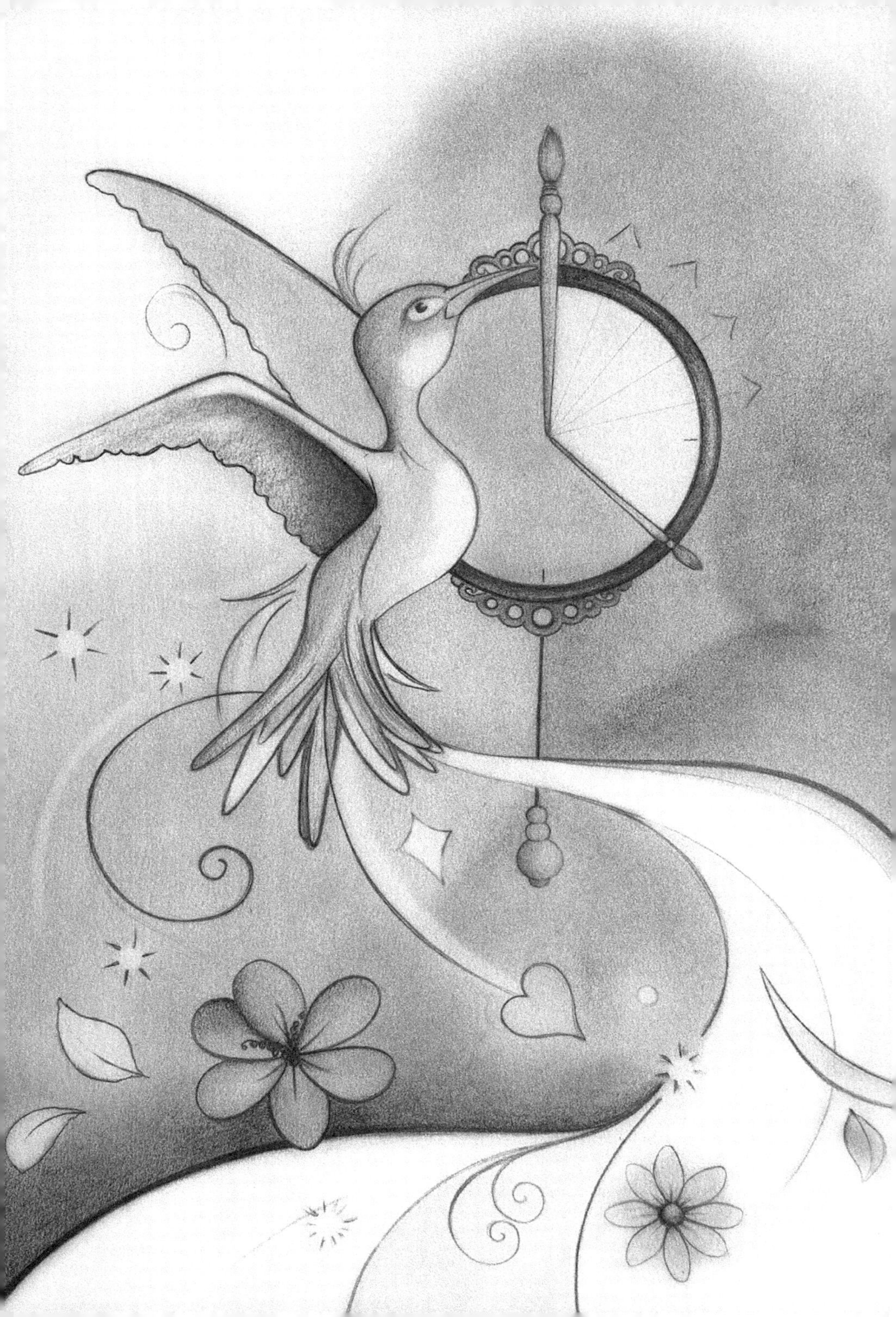

My Lens

I see
In colour, shape, brushstrokes and lines
In despair, and the lonely ticking of time
In random conversations, love and elation
In rich creative flow and grey desolation

Flying, soaring
Stumbling, crawling
Happy highs and deep lows
As fickle as the wind blows

Stained View

Was it worth it?
Did the sacrifice pay off?
You harbour so much hatred
So I guess maybe not

But you still have time
To redesign
The pattern of your life

Bitterness is an ugly friend
That haunts a spoon-fed mind
Empowerment could be yours
If you'd just draw the line

An open wound that festers
Your neglected child bleeds
Into ungrown manhood spiralling
Sowing rotten apple seeds

Tell me what to do
The line of your defence
But refuse all suggestions
Stay sitting on the fence

I have no more to offer
No energy for this game
When every dice you roll
Always lands the same

You you you
Stain the view, so askew
With entrenched negativity
So damn crazy blue

Snakes and Ladders

Watching, waiting, anticipating
Trying to stay three steps ahead
In this crazy game of theirs
Don't know which way to tread

Reliant, compliant, diminutively silent
Fervently nodding agreeably
Bending like a contortionist
So they'll deem to like me

Years of climbing ladders
And holding my breath tight
This fear of snakes and falling
Until death snuffs my light

A timed manipulation
Damn, I have been played
Booted down the serpent
They win, I can't be saved

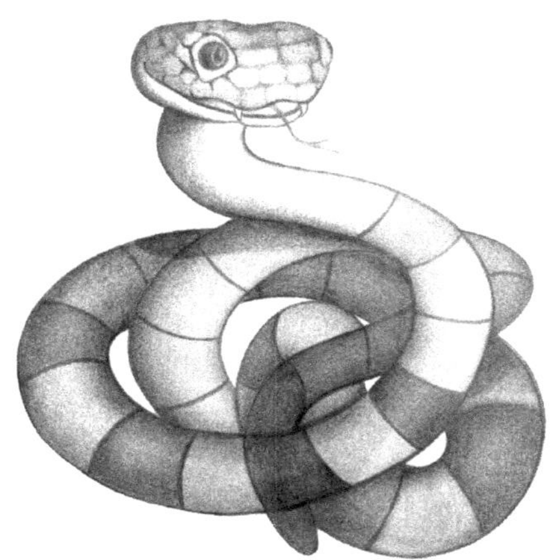

Ghost Gasping

The spiral of hatred leaves me gasping for air
Their smile dissolved to a cruel callous stare
No words, no explosion, no warning at all
Just a switch they flicked and walked out the door

I've been sitting here in dark purgatory
Lost and confused as to how this could be
Racing through memories that feel like a maze
Clinging to a bond, now suddenly erased

I have stifled my pain, kept it buried within
Endured the frost from their brutal ice wind
All stories have villains for dramatic effect
My name now sullied and I can't deflect

I have no agenda, no plan of attack
They struck first and I won't fight back
So I ghost walk the street of inner misery
'Til I learn, truly see, I am actually free

Will You Answer

What price will you finally pay?
The road to karma paved in clay

Excuses belittle you and me
Where is your priority?

Raging anger blinds your heart
Blood stains those you tore apart

Waiting, wilting, loathing grows
Is this the way our story goes?

Hollow Suspension

Look into my eyes
Please don't leave me hanging
Every choice past and present
Speared in hollow suspension

Where will the leaf fall?
Where will the car stall?
When will this stop hurting?
I'm so tired of not learning!

I've been waiting on you
Let you hold all the cards
Then wondered why my heart
Couldn't see shooting stars

Your eyes don't hold the answer
To the pain I hold within
The journey is on me
And it is time to begin

Guilty Milk

Can I take off this dress?
That makes me feel I am less
I just want to be me
For the world to see
Without fear or guilt
Over milk not yet spilt

Do I have to wear these heels?
Do you know how bad it feels?
My toes numb and mangled
Expectations tightly tangled
I just want to be me
For the world to see
Without fear or guilt
Over milk not yet spilt

I'll pour out the milk
And break this guilt
Get naked and raw
Never seen before
Me undecorated
Authentic, elated

Dark Closet Tumor

Hiding in dark safety
Never venturing out
Afraid to be open
Afraid to kick and shout
Here I am, see me
I want to be set free

My spirit slowly suffocated
The space cramped and cold
It is hard to breathe
And my story's not yet told
But I'm afraid to be open
Afraid to kick and shout
Here I am, see me
I want to be set free

I thought you locked me in
Your fear barred both the doors
That I was an innocent captive
Of your personality flaws
But I was afraid to be open
Afraid to kick and shout
Here I am, see me
I want to be set free

Being trapped was my decision
My own penalty
For letting self-judgement
Get the better of me
I don't want to be in the closet
I don't want to be afraid
I don't want to blame the outside
For the choices I have made

Dark closet tumor
Feasting on my mind
Creating the wrong message
Being so unkind
It is time to be open
Time to kick and shout
Here I am, see me
I choose to be free

Green

A twisting cloth wound too tight
Grotesque green and ready to fight
Wrestling jealousy invading my mind
I'm sucker punched and swinging blind

My inner voice yells, *Hey girl, no!*
Don't let jaded nastiness flow
Feelings of inferiority always win
When you let the green-eyed monster in

But quieting the beast that roars so loud
Sly and seductive, stubborn and proud
Is not an easy task to achieve
'Til loathing takes its cue to leave

I know how the whisper got in my head
It's burrowed deep and very well fed
Resetting the pattern takes strong affirmation
Self-awareness and pure determination

But I must change this societal wiring
Show my daughters sisterhood's firing
We need to make a collective stand
And fight the cause with a united hand

If we stay distracted feeling green
We cannot change the stage or scene

Push

Run 'til you can't breathe
Stomp 'til your thighs seize
Sing 'til your throat is hoarse
Swear 'til you lose your force
Cry 'til your red eyes ache
Fight 'til you conquer hate

Freedom is found
When you finally leap
Push through the fear
And you will reap

Standing Tall

Small doses they say
Like I'm too high a price to pay
They want me to be small
Swing the axe so I don't stand tall
Don't be loud, don't be bold
Just do as you are told
I've seen the ones that came before
Fire snuffed to a smoking bore
Gradually trained to compliant design
A withered flower drooped in resign
But I won't go down without a fight
I'll swerve left as they swerve right
I'll sing, write and paint my voice
Give myself another choice

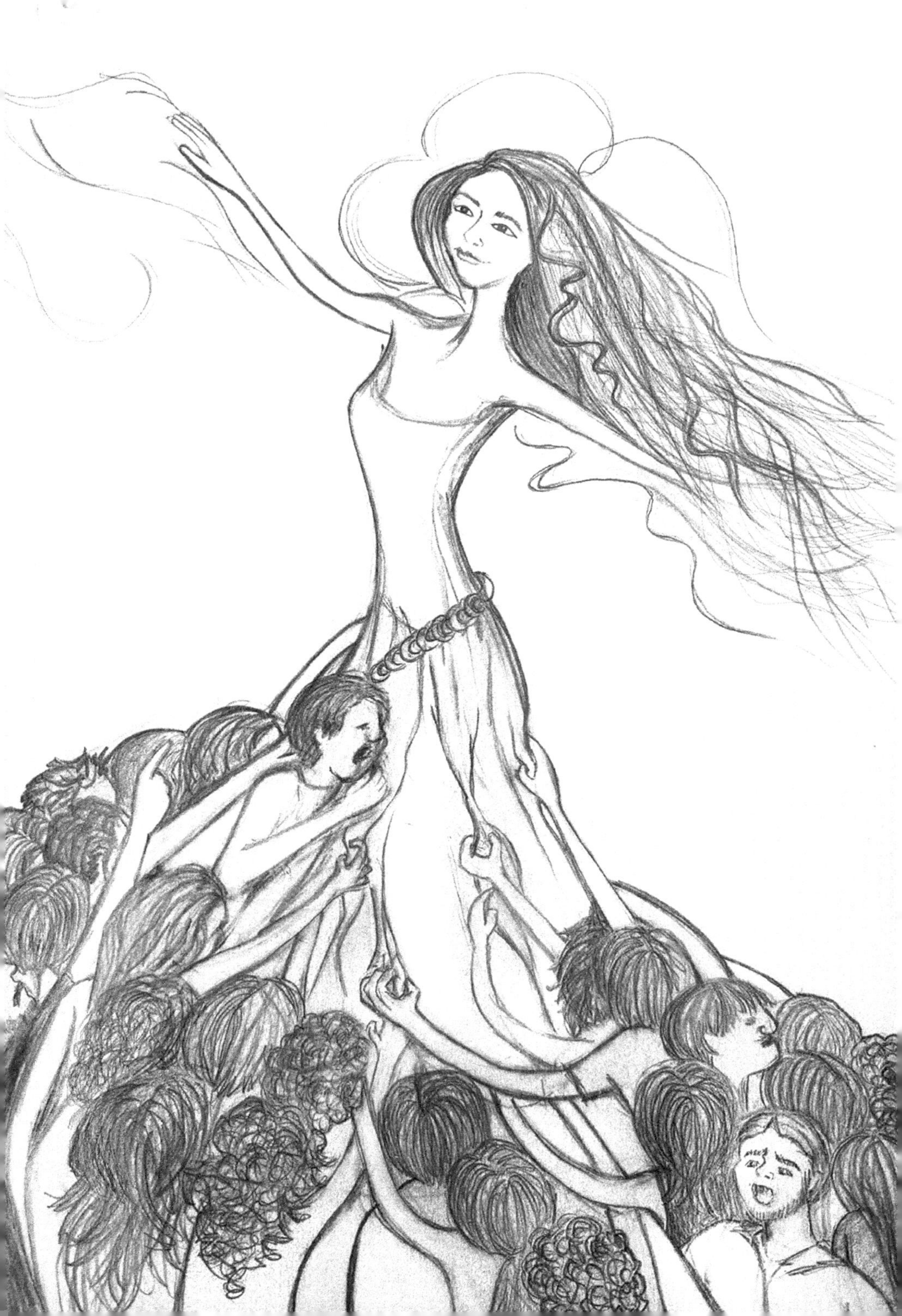

Malicious

Blindly navigating this minefield
Do I step or do I yield?

Spinning lies from jealous rage
Waging war won't keep me caged

Feeling inferior skews your view
Conspiring covertly, you stew in blue

Smile sweetly to fool the crowd
Conceal the knife beneath your shroud

Repeatedly stabbed, I take it all
But you will never see me fall

Lies in time will find the light
Luminate your malicious fight

I have a heart strong and true
I will not be destroyed by you

Your Path

If you only knew your talent
Was worth all the risk
To fight against the grain
And follow soulful bliss

Your choices build the tower
The mortar of your wall
Satisfying others
Will see it crash and fall

Appeasing is not the reason
To follow another's path
Love understands
What burns inside your heart

Each step you take is yours
To walk the path that's true
So your artistry and passion
Can paint the sky anew

Learning to Shine

True beauty elegantly stated
Should never be underestimated
Criticism is your demon fear
Calm bravery must resonate here
The form is not the image on TV
Tricking your mind so you can't see
You're losing your authenticity
To skeletal souless insincerity
The answer patiently is lying within
Free from imposed shame or sin
Shed the façade and expose your core
Feel the breeze as you begin to soar

Night Song

Restless is my ticking
As I fight, toss and kick
Conscious is my dreaming
A compulsive little tick

A delicate pretty whistle
Wakes the dark of night
Marking the new season
Its call a pure delight

I imagine she is tiny
With luminous black wings
Quick stepping on the branches
As she lifts her head and sings

I listen in the darkness
Distracted, far from sleep
Ignoring morning's coming
With duties I must keep

This moment is a treasure
That breaks the heavy mind
The sweetest sign of hope
A promise I must find

That even on this path
I can carve a piece of me
With confidence and truth
My sweet clarity

Every action of authenticity
Quiets my restless sleep
Sings the night bird's song
Claims a promise I must keep

Duality Casualty

Watch the one that's always smiling
Secretly she's downward spiralling

Creative, passionate, fiery, wild
Caged, clipped & cabinet filed

She is both and neither at the same time
Angry, deflated and needs a lifeline

Social politeness cling wraps her stare
The duality of persona-acutely aware!

One is truth and one is a pervading
Casualty of lies, ever cascading

She is both and neither, simultaneously
Sweetly smiling and needs to be free

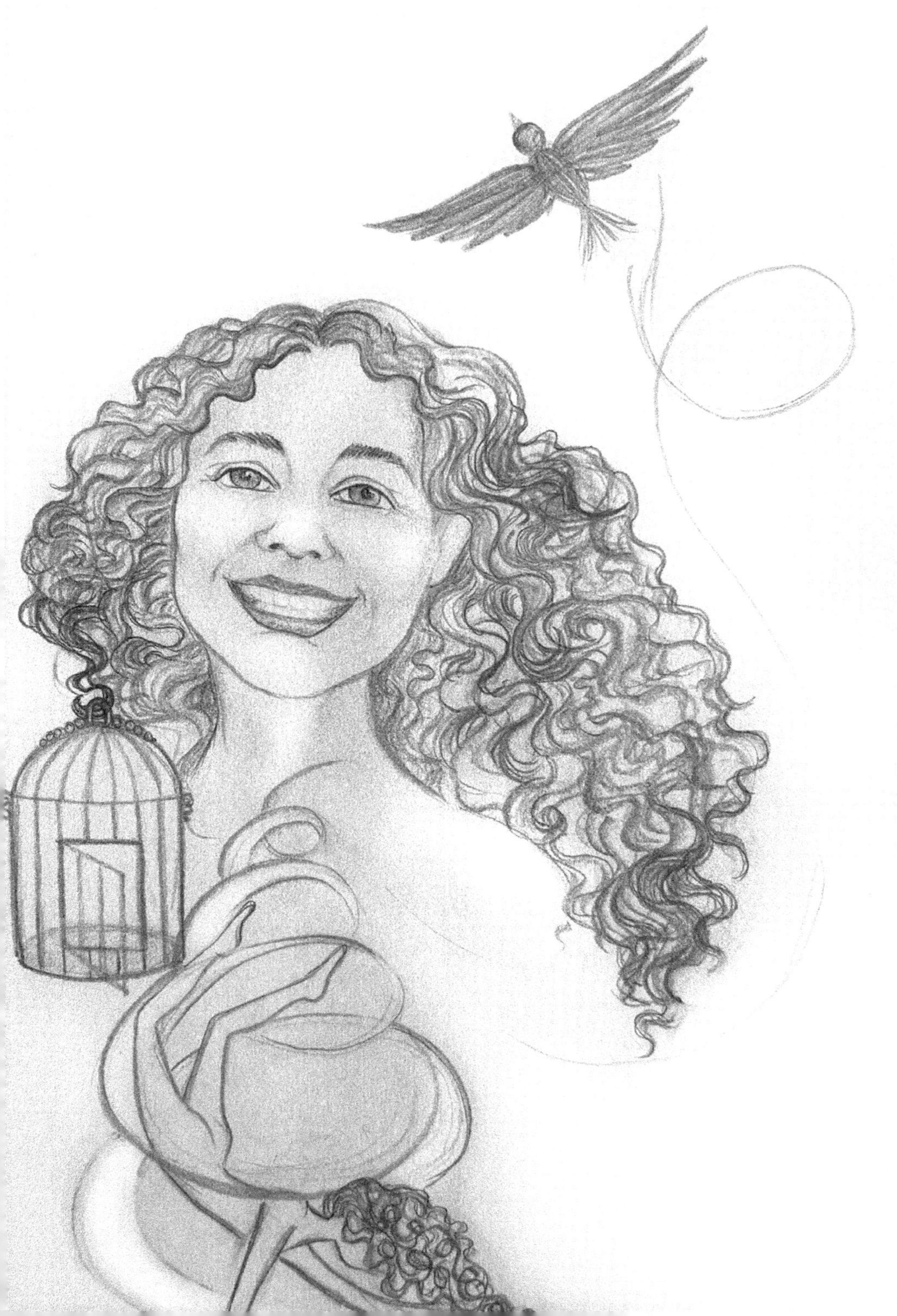